HIDE & BEAK

Georgia Angus

A guide to spotting Aussie birds in your backyard

Hardie Grant
EXPLORE

CONTENTS

BACKYARD BIRDS

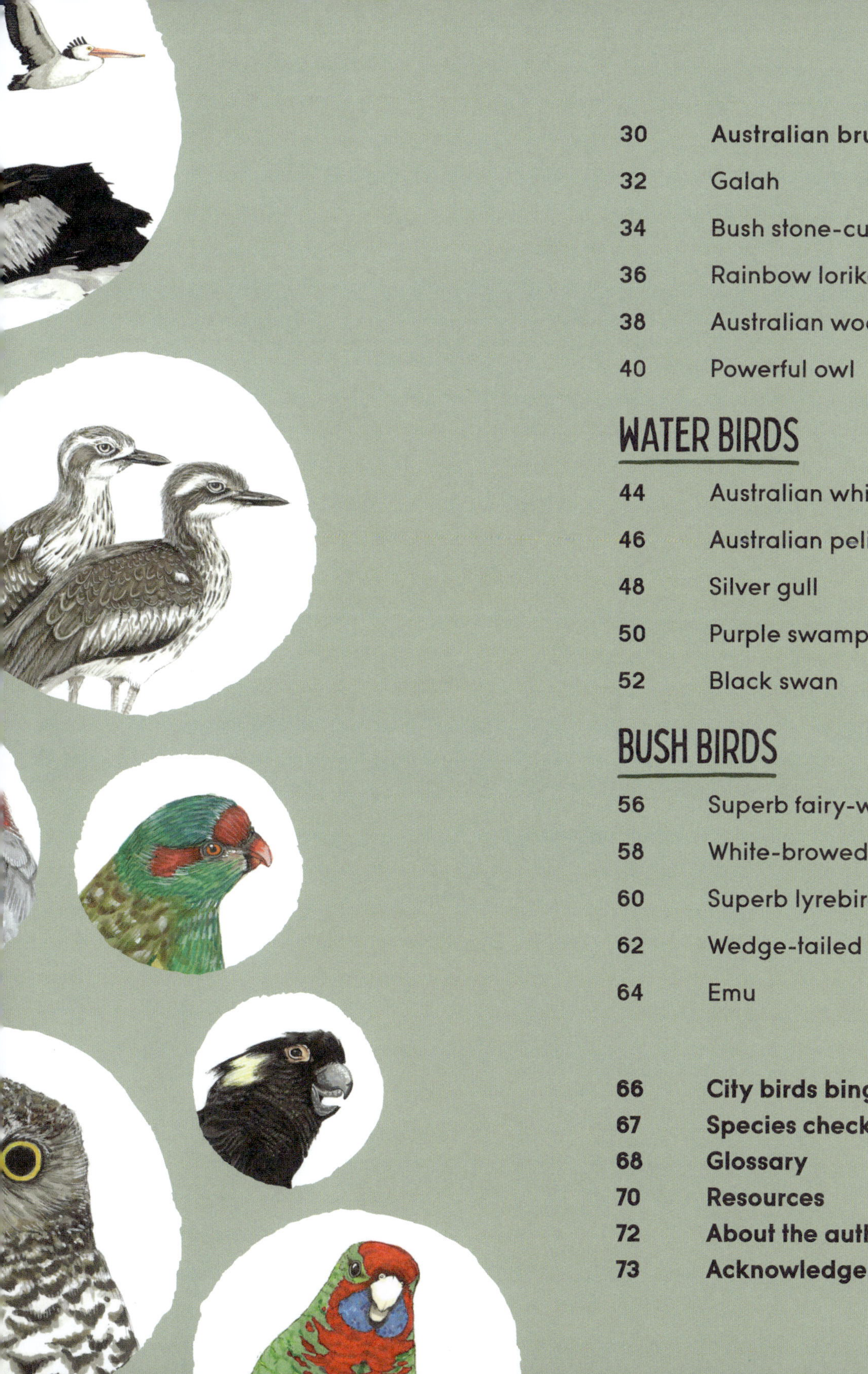

WATER BIRDS

BUSH BIRDS

INTRODUCTION

Birds are everywhere – if you take a look outside right now, you'll probably see one! They eat, hunt, hide and play around your home. Maybe you live in an apartment and your backyard is the city where seagulls and ravens perch on street lights. Or maybe you live in the suburbs where wattlebirds and magpies battle for territory in your garden. Or maybe you live in the country where wedge-tailed eagles circle overhead, hunting for rabbits. No matter where you are, birds will visit you – all you have to do is look for them!

There are about 11,000 bird species across the world, and in Australia we have around 800 native bird species. Some Australian birds live here all the time, some only spend half their time here, and others only occasionally visit Australia. Can you imagine flying thousands of kilometres each year between countries? The bar-tailed godwit flies over 10,000 kilometres from the northern hemisphere to Australia! What's even more amazing is that it doesn't take any breaks – it flies for more than a week non-stop. What a champion!

In this book, 30 of Australia's most common birds will introduce themselves to you. These are species you might encounter in your backyard, at the beach, in the city or in the bush.

You'll meet tiny birds, like the white-browed scrubwren who lives in thickets and shrubs, eating insects and gossiping with other scrubwrens. You'll meet big birds like the patient emu whom you might see ambling around the bush, looking for seeds and insects to eat. You'll meet noisy birds like the sulphur-crested cockatoo and secretive birds like the tawny frogmouth. Whatever kind of bird you're interested in, you'll meet them here!

They all have clever ways of finding everything they need. Birds have changed – or adapted – so they can survive in the places

EASTERN WHIPBIRD

they live (the environment). For example, the peregrine falcon lives on mountain cliffs or over farmland, but it can also live in the city where it nests on high buildings, hunting pigeons instead of ducks and songbirds. The welcome swallow has also adapted, building its nests under people's roofs, and living off the insects that fly around in the air above the suburbs.

I wrote this book so that you can learn about different birds that may visit your backyard. When you see these birds, they will also be teaching you things about their habitat. You can use this book to help you figure out what bird you've seen at home, or out on your adventures. You'll find that you'll quickly get better at seeing, hearing and recognising different types of birds.

Some entries include the bird's name from three First Nations languages: Alyawarr, Gumbaynggirr and Taungurung. These are only examples from the many First Nations languages that are spoken across the continent. Along with species information, you will find a QR code that your parent or guardian can scan using their phone. This will take you to a recording of the bird call for that entry, so you can listen as well as read! Each entry also includes my illustrations of these beautiful animals.

So, let's start learning about how amazing birds are!

PEREGRINE FALCON

SUPERB LYREBIRD

PACKING TO GO BIRDWATCHING

TIPS

- Take someone with you
- Check the forecast
- Carry extra water and food

WHAT ARE BIRDS?

Birds are dinosaurs. It might be hard to believe, but it's true! All modern birds are descendants of the dinosaurs that walked the earth millions of years ago. Some dinosaurs grew feathers before they started to look anything like birds, and then over many, many years they developed the ability to fly. So today we still have little dinosaurs flying all around us! How cool is that?

Birds all hatch from eggs, and have a beak and wings. They all need water to drink and wash in, food to eat, and places to shelter and nest. Not every bird flies, but all birds have one thing that no other animal has: feathers.

Feathers help birds in different ways. Down feathers help keep birds warm, while filoplume feathers help birds sense their surroundings. Tail and wing feathers are strong enough to create resistance, helping birds to fly.

Birds come in different sizes, shapes and colours, and have evolved to face different challenges. There are songbirds, like magpies and lyrebirds. There are waterbirds, like ducks, pelicans and seagulls There are birds of prey, like eagles and owls, and so many others.

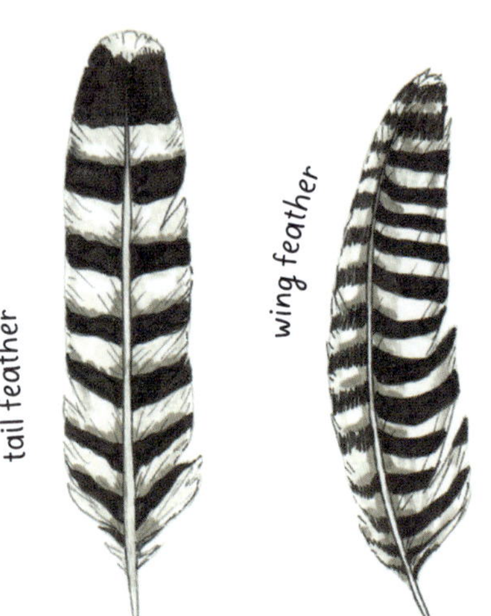

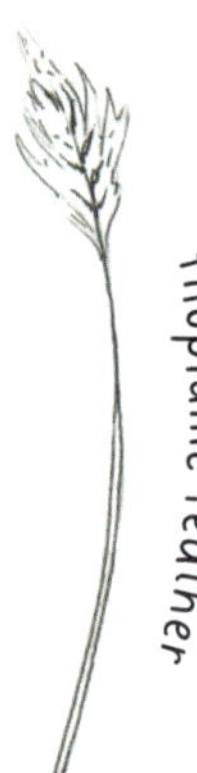

Most birds use their wings to fly, while others walk on strong legs instead of flying (emus and cassowaries) or use their wings to swim (penguins). These birds all have unique characteristics because species need different things – say, a certain body type, or certain skills – to survive in different habitats. For example, a bird that lives in an area with lots of fish is going to survive better if it can use a big, stretchy beak to scoop those fish out of the water, like the Australian pelican. A bird like the cassowary lives in thick forest, so it needs strong legs to be able to walk long distances all day through trees, searching for fruit to eat.

Knowing what all birds have in common helps us to appreciate the differences between them, and how those differences help them fit perfectly in different ecosystems. In these pages you'll find some information about basic bird anatomy (the names for different body parts), with illustrations of feet and beaks. You will see how different these body parts look, depending on what a bird is using them for.

SOUTHERN CASSOWARY

LITTLE PENGUIN

BIRD BODIES

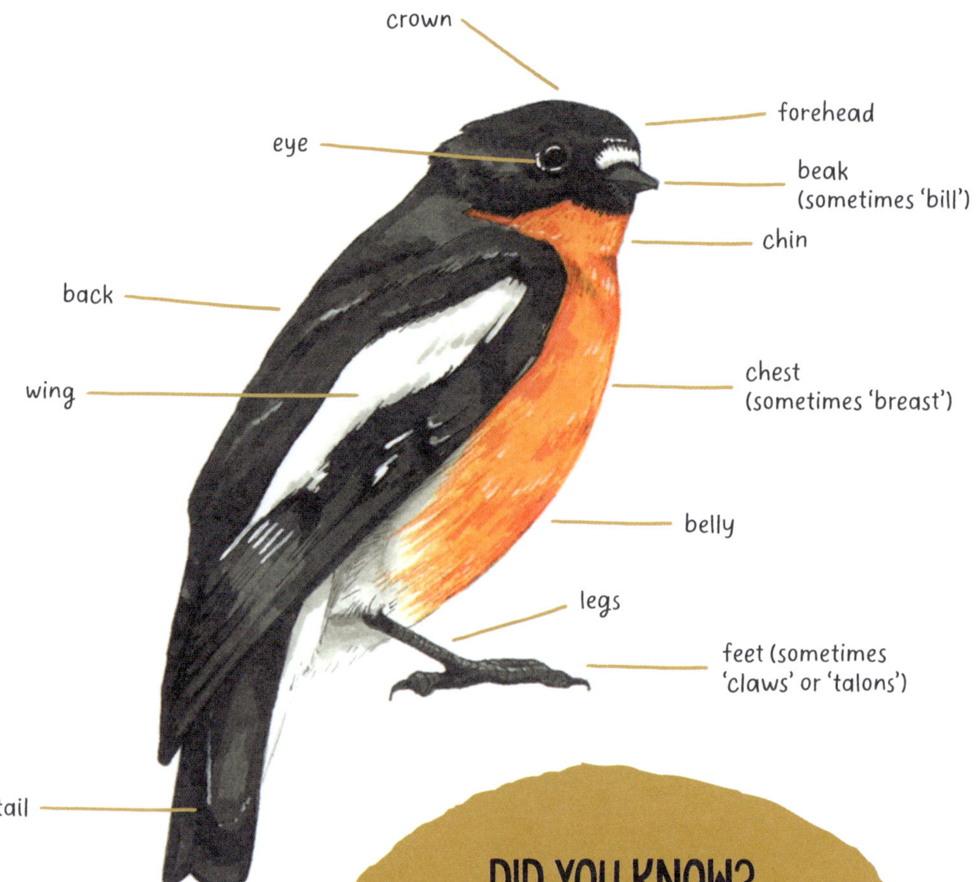

DID YOU KNOW?

Around the world, there are 60 species of birds that can't fly, including penguins, ostriches and kiwis. Some birds can fly but not very well! Have you ever seen a chicken flapping around? They can only get about two or three metres off the ground, and only for short bursts. They'd still beat a penguin in a flying competition though!

BEAKS & FEET

seed eater
fly grabber
mud prober
rabbit hunter
skink catcher
nectar sipper
nectar lapper
worm extractor
fruit muncher
frog snatcher
wader foot
owl talon
kingfisher feet
eagle talon
songbird foot
duck foot
cassowary claw
falcon talon
penguin foot

BIRDS' NESTS AND EGGS

While nearly all birds make nests, they come in many different shapes and styles, from a simple cleared patch on the ground to a complex nest made of twigs and spiderwebs, or raft nests of folded reeds.

Nests are made to keep eggs safe so the baby birds can hatch in a protected environment. Birds choose to make nests a certain way depending on the habitat they live in, and the kinds of predators that are nearby.

Some birds nest in several different ways depending on what's available in their habitat. For example, kingfishers sometimes nest in tree hollows, and sometimes in a burrow they've dug into the riverbank. Sometimes they will even nest in termite mounds! The termites just accept the invasion and build a barrier around the birds' nesting chamber to protect themselves from more damage. This creates the perfect environment for incubating the kingfisher's eggs, as the termites carefully control the temperature of the mound.

In the nest are the eggs. Baby birds grow inside eggs, then hatch when they are strong enough. Eggs are made up of an embryo (which grows into the chick) and the egg white and yolk (made up of proteins, fats and other nutrients), which feeds the chick as it grows. The hard outer shell of the egg protects the chick until it grows big enough to hatch. The shell keeps unwanted germs out, but is porous, so it allows oxygen in.

RAFT NEST

DID YOU KNOW?

Eggs vary a lot in size and colour. Some birds will lay only one egg a year, such as the superb lyrebird. Other birds, like the Australian wood duck, can lay 11 eggs per year!

INSIDE AN EGG

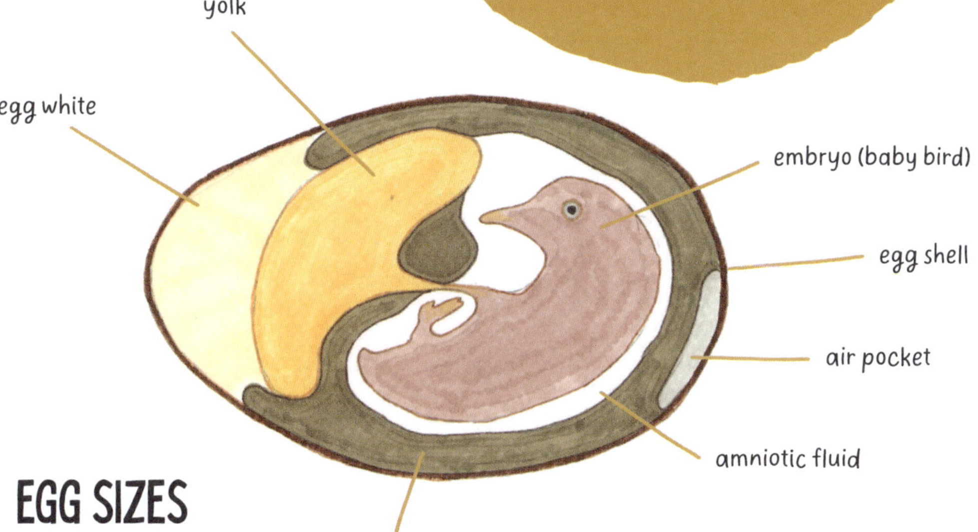

EGG SIZES

TYPES OF BIRD NESTS

Classic cup nest (made by many songbirds)

Wineglass cup nest (made by fantails)

Urban mud nest (made by swallows)

Cup-shaped mud nest (made by choughs, magpie larks)

Special dome nest (made by yellow-rumped thornbills)

DID YOU KNOW?

Some very clever birds like the careful yellow-rumped thornbill will make secret entrances to their nests. They even build a decoy 'cup' on the top of their nest to distract any predators trying to get at their eggs!

Raft nest (made by water-dwelling birds, like purple swamphens)
Dome nest (made by thornbills, scrubwrens, fairy-wrens and other small bush birds)
Scrape nest (made by ground-dwelling birds, like emus and lapwings)
Tree-hollow nest (used by most parrots and cockatoos, kookaburras and many other birds)
Tunnel nest (made by some kingfishers, rainbow bee-eaters and pardalotes)

BIRD SIZES

How big are the birds in this book?

wedge-tailed eagle
welcome swallow
Australian pelican
red wattlebird
crimson rosella
Australian
brushturkey
Australian magpie
white-browed
scrubwren
emu
crested pigeon
pied currawong
white-faced heron
superb fairy-wren
silver gull
eastern spinebill

HOW TO BIRDWATCH

Did you know that there are different kinds of birdwatchers?

There are casual birdwatchers – people who just like to notice birds when they happen to see them. Then there are 'birders' – people who like to go looking for birds, and often make lists of what they see on a bird walk. Birders often keep a 'life list', which includes every bird they've ever seen.

And finally there are 'twitchers' – the most hardcore kind of birdwatcher. These are really dedicated birdwatchers who always want to add new species of birds to their life list.

If an exotic bird from overseas accidentally winds up in remote Australia, some birdwatchers will get on planes, trains and cars just to get a glimpse of that special species.

If you find yourself wanting to do this, you're a twitcher!

Usually, the best way to birdwatch is to notice birds when you're visiting somewhere nice with your family or friends. You could start by looking in your backyard, the local park, or on your next visit to the beach. If you're lucky, you may get a chance to go to other special places in Australia, like rainforests, lakes, rivers, mountains or deserts. In all these places you can see different types of birds.

Once you spot a bird, make sure you're in a safe place to pause and look at it (don't stop when crossing the road, or on a busy footpath). Take your time to really look at the bird and notice its details. How big is the beak? What colour are the feathers? Are there any patterns on it? Does it have a long or short tail?

If you're lucky enough to have a pair of binoculars, you can use them to get a closer look. Noticing those little details will help you to figure out the species. Sometimes you may hear the bird calling, which can also be helpful. Most field guides (like this book!) have a description of a bird's call to help you figure out which bird you saw.

Once you've noticed a few details about the bird, you can look at your field guide to try to figure out what its name is. Start by trying to find birds that look like the one you saw, noting them down. Then use other details to narrow your options. Look at the map – did you see this bird in a place in the coloured part of the map? You can also look at the habitat you're in. Does it match the habitat in the species description?

Then you can use extra details – like colour, beak size, patterns and tail shape – to confirm which species you saw. Even if you're not sure exactly which species it was, you'll learn a lot by trying to narrow it down, and you'll have a better chance at figuring it out when you see that bird again!

It takes a little while to recognise a species, but once you learn a bird you rarely forget it! So take your time. If you want to, keep a list so you know how many different species you've seen (you can start with the checklist on page 67). This is one way to start birdwatching, but you will also learn a lot by simply spending time in nature, and by looking at and listening to what's happening around you. If you're being patient, soon enough you will start to notice birds wherever you go.

This book is a good starting place for you to learn some common birds. In time, when you get to know these birds better, you may want to use a bigger field guide, which lists all of the bird species in Australia. This will help you to learn more as you start to visit places farther from home.

Seeing a new bird species is so exciting, and every new bird has something to tell you about the environment. All you have to do is look and listen. Good luck!

DID YOU KNOW?

Binoculars have a small knob between the eyepieces to help you focus. If the bird looks blurry, spin the knob until it becomes clearer. Happy birdwatching!

HELPING BIRDS

While it's great fun to watch birds, it's important to know that bird numbers around the world are dropping at an alarming rate, and many species are now critically endangered or extinct. Climate change, habitat loss and pollution have harmed birds' health, and so they need our help.

This is where you come in! If we all make some small changes, we can help our feathered friends to be healthy and strong, making sure they have places to live, wash, feed and nest.

Here are some simple ways you can help birds:

- Plant native shrubs and grasses in your backyard. The best plants for native birds are spiky, dense bushes that have lots of hiding places. You can also encourage your neighbours to grow some native plants, so your street becomes a habitat corridor. This gives birds and other native animals a safe 'path' which they can use to move around between people's backyards.
- Put a birdbath in your garden. This can be as simple as buying a wide salad bowl from an op shop and filling it with water. The best place to put a birdbath is close to some bushes, which helps little birds feel safe while they wash. You can even put in multiple birdbaths, so that big birds and little birds have options to choose from. Your backyard can become a day spa for birds! But make sure you clean and refill your birdbath every couple of days. No one wants a dirty bath!
- Look after your local trees. Without large trees for nesting, many birds stop coming to an area. Tree hollows can take 100 years to form! That means every old-growth tree

in your neighbourhood is very precious. Make sure that your local trees are healthy, and that your neighbours know about how much habitat they provide to local birds, possums, sugar gliders and other animals. All these creatures call trees home, sweet home!

- Join your local Landcare group. Many volunteers across the country spend a couple of hours a month weeding and planting native plants. Joining a Landcare group can be a great way not only to look after local birds, but also to learn about the bushland you're working on.
- Tell your family and friends to only use owl-safe rat poisons (see p. 70 for a guide).
- Take part in citizen science projects like the Aussie Backyard Bird Count, which happens every October. You count every bird you can see in 20 minutes. All this information helps conservation scientists know which birds are doing well across the country, and which birds need help. You can also submit your birdwatching lists to eBird, or you can add interesting sightings onto the Atlas of Living Australia. (See Resources on p. 70 for more information.)

IT'S TIME TO MEET SOME BIRDS!
LET'S START WITH SOME SPECIES YOU MIGHT SEE IN OR NEAR YOUR BACKYARD. THESE BIRDS LIVE IN PARKS AND BUSHLAND AROUND OUR HOMES, AND SOMETIMES VISIT OUR HOUSES. HOW MANY DO YOU RECOGNISE?

Backyard Birds

ARRPWER

[are-POOR]
(Alyawarr)

NGAAMBUL

[ngahm-bool]
(Gumbaynggirr)

BARWANG

[bar-wang]
(Taungurung)

DID YOU KNOW?

In springtime, when female magpies start to nest, males can get very aggressive defending their territory. They will even swoop people who are coming too close to their nests. Watch out!

Spot the difference: Can you spot the differences between me and the magpie-lark?

AUSTRALIAN MAGPIE

Gymnorhina tibicen

ABOUT ME

I'm a smart bird who likes to spend my days on people's lawns, hunting for earthworms. When I stalk across the lawn, you might see me turn my head to listen. My hearing is so sensitive that I can hear grubs moving in the soil under the grass, so I know where to dig with my beak. I'm omnivorous, eating mostly earthworms and grubs (beetle larvae), but I sometimes scavenge food scraps from humans.

I stay on the same patch of lawn or parkland for many years, and I'm very territorial. If other birds come onto my patch I usually chase them away.

I live with the same partner my whole life, and my young chicks stay with me until they're old enough to go and find a partner and their own territory.

LOOK

I live all over Australia, but I'm most common in backyards and parks where there are plenty of grassy lawns full of my favourite food – worms!

LISTEN

My best-known call is a warbling song that I make in the morning and at dusk. I often sing with other members of my family, as if we are a choir. I also give a harsh warning call, *kwaargh*, which I usually make when someone is intruding on my territory.

I can also mimic many sounds I hear around my home, including other birds, dogs, sirens and even human speech. I'm always listening to the sounds around me, especially the songs of other birds, which tell me about what's going on in my neighbourhood.

DJIIN DJIIN

[djiin djiin,
'dj' as in 'da**ng**er']
(Taungurung)

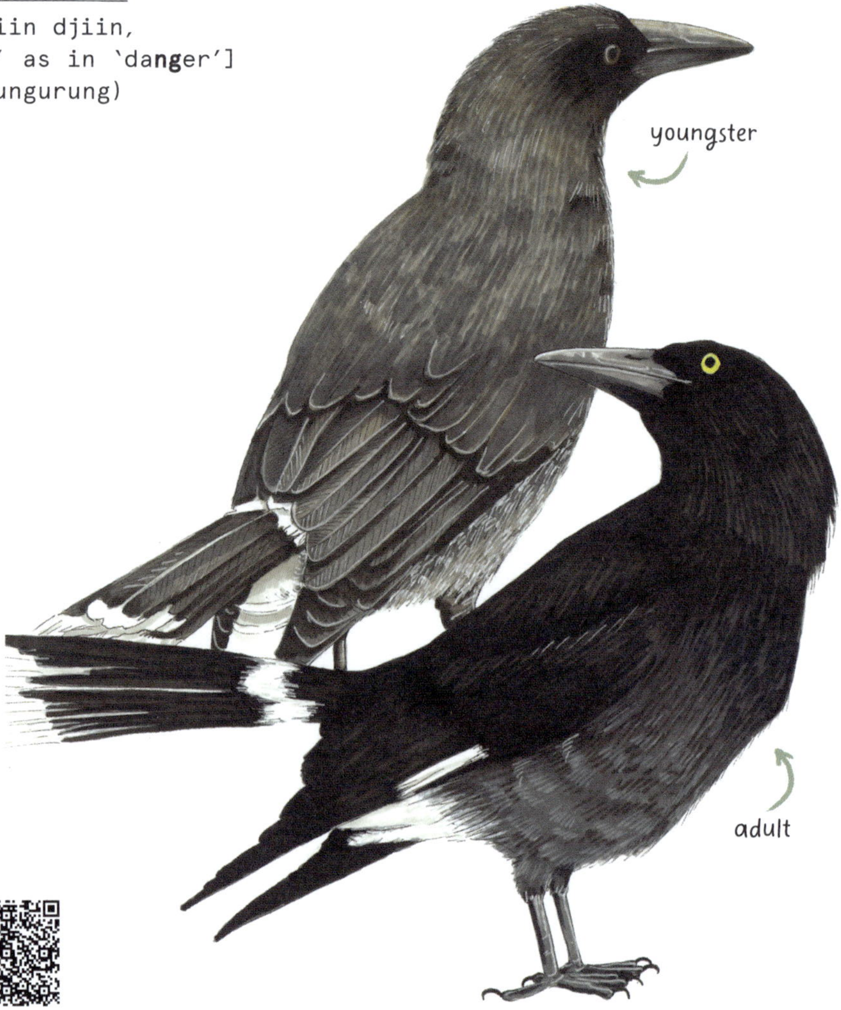
youngster
adult

Spot the difference: Can you spot the differences between me and my close relative, the grey currawong?

pied
grey

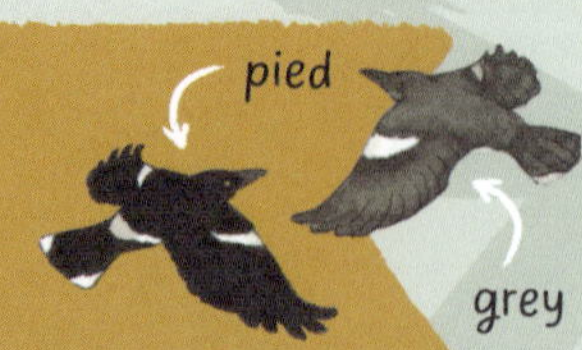

PIED CURRAWONG

Strepera graculina

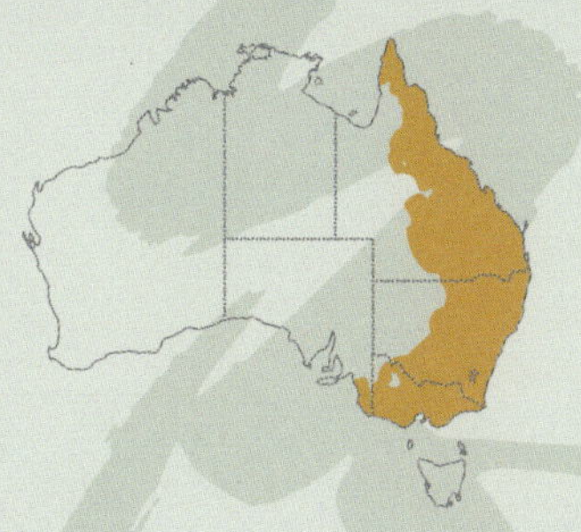

ABOUT ME

I'm a large black and white bird that sometimes gets mistaken for an Australian magpie (*see* p. 2). I have striking yellow eyes which are an easy way to tell me apart from a magpie, which has red eyes.

I have a beautiful call, but sometimes other birds are wary of me because I like to steal eggs and chicks from other birds' nests. I don't care what the bird is! I'll steal from birds as small as thornbills to birds as big as superb lyrebirds.

I'm an omnivore, so I eat both meat (like skinks and insects) and plants (like fruits and seeds). Sometimes I steal dog biscuits from a dog's bowl, and fruit from people's backyard trees. Raspberries and figs are some of my favourite treats.

LOOK

I live in backyards, parks and the bush. Because I eat a wide variety of foods, I can adapt to many different environments.

Sometimes I live in the same place all year round, but sometimes my fellow currawongs and I choose to holiday for the summer up in the mountains where it's cooler. Then we move down to the lowlands for winter to stay a bit warmer. So you may find that one day you have a big flock of currawongs arrive in your area to settle in for the season.

LISTEN

I make lots of different calls, though my most memorable call is a frog-like gurgle. I also make a whistle that goes from high to low, a bit like a sigh, *qwoop-qwaaaa*.

DURARONG

[du-ra-rong]
(Taungurung)

Spot the difference: Can you spot the differences between me and the sacred kingfisher? We're both kingfishers, and we sometimes live in the same areas.

LAUGHING KOOKABURRA

Dacelo novaeguineae

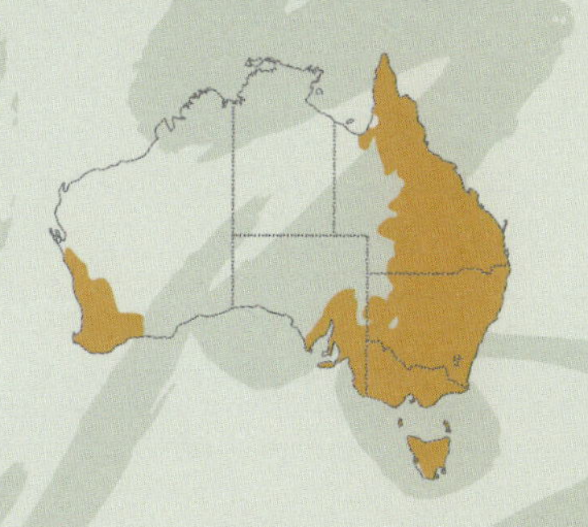

ABOUT ME

I'm part of the bird family known as 'kingfishers'. Although I rarely dive into the water for fish, I do dive from tree branches to catch small lizards and insects, like I'm fishing on dry land.

I enjoy spending time with other kookaburras, and usually keep the same partner my whole life. My species uses tree hollows for nests, where we can safely lay our eggs and feed our babies when they hatch.

I like to eat reptiles, including snakes and lizards, particularly skinks. I will also eat insects, grubs and worms.

LOOK

I usually live in parklands, open bushland and suburbs where there are lots of tall gum trees to rest in. Try going to your local park or creek and listen for a loud laugh! Sometimes I sit quietly on branches looking for food on the ground below, so don't forget to look up.

LISTEN

My name comes from my call, which sounds like someone laughing loudly, *koo-kah-kah-kah*. When I'm young, it takes me some time to learn to laugh properly, so you may hear me practising my wheezy chuckle. You can often hear me calling in the mornings and evenings.

YANGGAK

[yang-gak]
(Taungurung)

youngster

adult
(view from
below)

adult

Spot the difference: Can you spot the differences between me and another honeyeater, the noisy friarbird?

RED WATTLEBIRD

Anthochaera carunculata

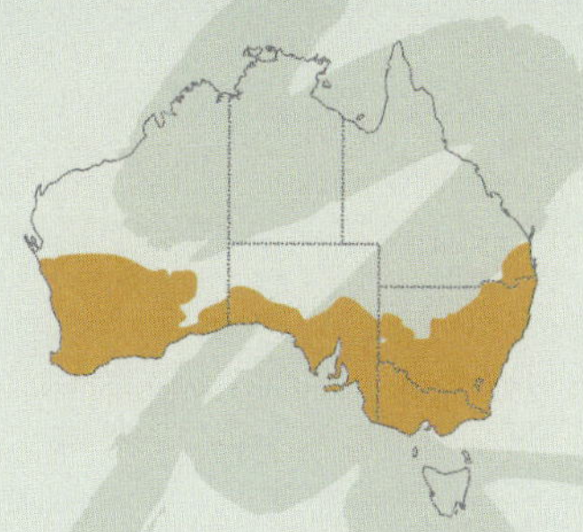

ABOUT ME

I'm one of Australia's largest honeyeaters. My family are named 'honeyeaters' because we mostly eat sugary sweet nectar from flowers, which gives us lots of energy. Some of my favourite flowering plants are banksias, grevilleas and gum trees. My name comes from the red wattles (small dangly things), which you can see on both sides of my neck.

When I'm feeding I angrily defend my flowers from other birds that come nearby. I chase off smaller birds, like the Eastern spinebill (*see* p. 12) and other small honeyeaters to make sure that I have all the nectar to myself. I also eat insects, which are rich in protein.

When it comes time to breed, I make a cup-shaped nest from sticks and grasses, and line it with downy feathers. This is where I lay my eggs.

LOOK

I love living in the suburbs, and in open bushland with plenty of flowering plants. Try looking for me in gardens with lots of native flowers, or in your local park.

LISTEN

I make a harsh *charck*, often early in the morning. I also sometimes make a rattling call, and snap my beak loudly.

adult

youngster

Spot the difference: Can you spot the differences between me and my close relative, the bell miner?

NOISY MINER

Manorina melanocephala

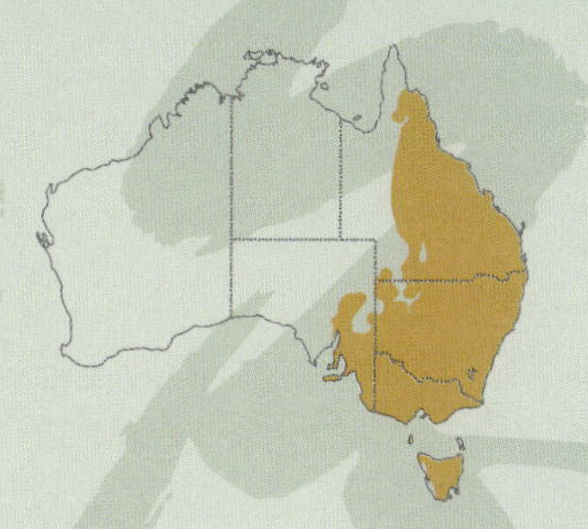

ABOUT ME

I'm a very talkative and noisy bird, and I spend most of my time moving around the tree canopy, looking for nectar. I sometimes also eat insects and fruit.

You may notice me looking for flowers on gum trees, banksias or grevilleas. I love nectar so much, that, like the red wattlebird (*see* p. 9), I aggressively defend any flowers I find, and chase other birds away. I also swoop humans during my breeding season. Some might say I'm the meanest bird there is!

When nesting, I make a cup-shaped nest high in a tree. My family and friends all help me raise my chicks. We work as a group to make sure everyone else stays away. No wonder we come across as mean!

LOOK

I live in eastern Australia among the eucalypts of suburbs and cities. I used to only live in dry, open woodland without much ground cover (no shrubs and bushes where little birds can hide). Now that suburbs and cities tend to only have a few big trees, this has become the perfect place for me to thrive. I can dominate an area from the treetops, and little birds have nowhere to hide from my attacks.

LISTEN

I most often make a loud, repetitive *yip, yip, yip* call. But if someone enters my territory, or there is a threat nearby, I make an alarm call – a rising *qweepp*. Usually the whole flock makes this call together to scare our enemies.

youngster

adult

adult

DID YOU KNOW?

The spinebill is one of the few Australian birds that can hover, a bit like a hummingbird. Their wings beat so fast, they become a blur. Imagine being able to move your body that fast! (Go on, give it a try!)

EASTERN SPINEBILL

Acanthorhynchus tenuirostris

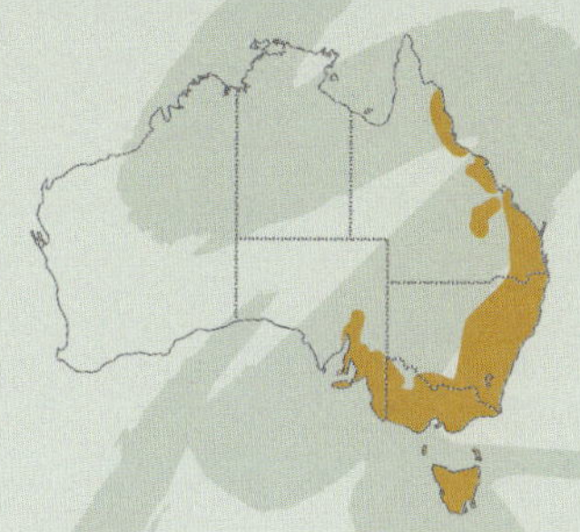

ABOUT ME

I'm a tiny, super-fast honeyeater, named for my long beak, which looks a bit like the sharp spine you might find on a spiky bush. My favourite food is nectar, which is why you'll see me buzzing around flowering shrubs. My long, curved bill helps me sip nectar from the bottom of flowers – it's like my own built-in straw!

I also help the flowers I drink from. When I sip the nectar, I brush up against the flower's anthers (see illustration below), and get pollen all over my forehead! Then when I visit another flower, some of that old pollen is transferred into the new flower. This allows a seed to germinate and grow. So sometimes it pays to be a messy eater!

When it comes time to breed, I make a cup-shaped nest of twigs, grass and spiderwebs in a tree.

LOOK

I live in eastern Australia (though I have a close relative, the western spinebill, who lives in Western Australia). Flowering plants are my main food source, so I like areas of native bushland with lots of dense plants. That way, I can dart around, drink from flowers, then get back to the safety of nearby shrubs.

LISTEN

I make a high-pitched, rapid-fire whistle *whii-whii-whii-whii-whii-whii-whii*. My wings also make a distinctive *purr* when I fly past.

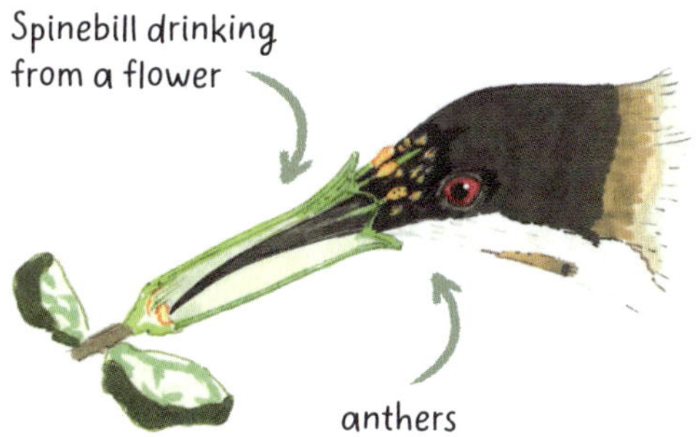

ITETHERR-ITETHERR

[i-TITTH-er i-titth-er]
(Alyawarr)

GANYJARR-GANYJARR

[gun-jar-gun-jar]
(Gumbaynggirr)

DJIRRI DJIRRI

[djirr-i djirr-i,
'dj' as in 'da**ng**er']
(Taungurung)

Spot the difference: Can you spot the differences between me and my relative, the grey fantail?

WILLIE WAGTAIL

Rhipidura leucophrys

ABOUT ME

I'm a brave little bird who gets my name from the distinctive way I wag my tail from side to side. (Humans haven't figured out why I do this, and I'm not telling!)

I'm a very good flier, and if you watch me closely, you may see me twisting and turning in the air as I chase insects, which are my main food source.

I'm a very bold and curious bird, so I often call out to people who come into my territory, warning them off. I attack birds who are much bigger than me (like kookaburras, p. 7) if they intrude on my territory, or threaten my chicks.

LOOK

You might see me hanging out in farmland or near open grassy areas in parks or sports ovals. These are places where it's easy for me to hunt flying insects. Even though I like these open areas, I also need good cover and native bushland nearby so I can nest, shelter and find a variety of other insects.

LISTEN

I make a clear, slightly haughty *jikirty-jik-jik*. I can also give a rattling warning call.

IRRWEK-IRRWEK PWELKER
[i-ROOK i-rook POOL-ker]
(Alyawarr)

Spot the difference: Can you spot the differences between me and another native pigeon, the common bronzewing?

CRESTED PIGEON

Ocyphaps lophotes

ABOUT ME

I'm a good-looking pigeon with a pointy spike of feathers on my head. From far away I look grey, but up close you might see purple, green and blue feathers on my wings when the sunlight hits them.

I like to spend time in large groups of fellow crested pigeons, mostly on grassy lawns in parks and backyards. I sometimes feed in a flock with other seed-eating birds, including spotted doves, corellas and galahs (especially if humans are feeding us!).

When looking for a mate, the male of my species fans out his tail and bobs his head up and down, cooing. When it comes time to nest, I build a messy structure of twigs in a tree. We both share in incubating and raising our young.

LOOK

Try looking for me in your suburb near parks and picnic grounds. I need trees to retreat to and nest in, although I sometimes build my nests in thick cypress hedges or in shrubs. I often hang out on powerlines where I can get a good view of everything around me. Some might even call it a bird's-eye view!

LISTEN

Sometimes when I'm with fellow pigeons, I make a soft, repeated *coo*. But my best-known 'call' is the loud whistling noise that special feathers on my wings make when I get spooked and fly away. This noise also warns other birds that danger is near, usually causing them to flee too.

Spot the difference: Can you spot the differences between me and the little corella? We are both cockatoos.

SULPHUR-CRESTED COCKATOO

Cacatua galerita

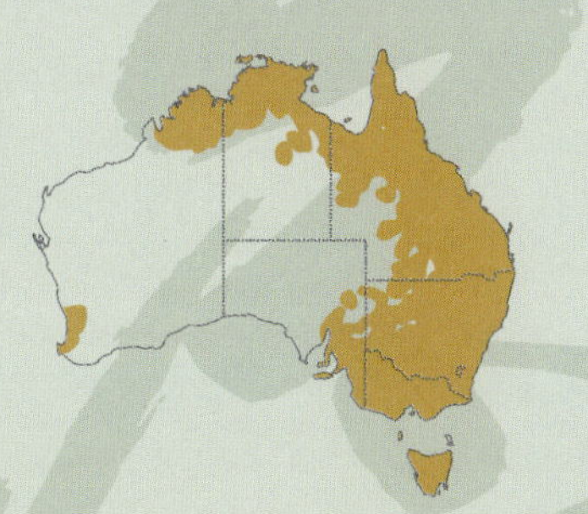

ABOUT ME

I'm a boisterous and noisy parrot that you can easily recognise by my bright yellow crest. I can lift or drop this crest, depending on whether I'm feeling playful or angry or happy. I usually spend my time in big flocks and I love to swoop around chaotically, even flying in loop-the-loops and screeching as I fly. It's great fun!

If I'm bored I sometimes chew on outdoor furniture or roof gutters. While I may seem silly, I'm actually a very smart bird. I'm good at problem-solving, especially when it comes to scoring some tucker! I can open bin lids to get at food scraps, and in some places you might see me operating water fountains to help myself to a drink! How clever am I?

My preferred food is seeds from either native or introduced species. I like to graze on grass seeds on the ground, feed on gumnuts, and tear open pine cones with my strong hooked beak. I also like to eat fruit, some flowers and some insects.

LOOK

I live over lots of Australia, except dry arid areas in the middle of the country. I particularly like areas of open forest with big trees that have hollows for me to nest in.

LISTEN

I make a really loud screeching – *screaaargh*! If I call right nearby, you might want to cover your ears!

ANGERL

[u-NGERL]
['U' as in 'CL**U**MP' or 'ER**U**PT']
(Alyawarr)

WAANG

[waang, 'aa' as in 'c**ar**t']
(Taungurung)

Spot the difference: Can you spot the differences between me and another black bird, the white-winged chough?

AUSTRALIAN RAVEN

Corvus coronoides

ABOUT ME

Although people sometimes call me a crow, I'm actually one of three different species of ravens found in Australia. To make things even more confusing, Australia has two species of crows as well! There's not really that much difference between a crow and a raven, unless you want to get technical, but we all live in slightly different areas. I'm the most common raven in Sydney, Canberra and Perth.

I spend a lot of my time hanging out with small groups of ravens, looking for food. I'm a very smart bird and I steal food from wherever I can get it. I have even learned how to unzip hikers' packs to steal their snacks!

I eat a huge variety of things, including fruit and seeds, but I prioritise meat where I can get it. I often catch lizards, large insects, frogs and small birds in bushland areas, and I steal eggs and chicks from other birds' nests to eat. In urban areas, I also feed from rubbish bins and steal food scraps. I'm not fussy!

LOOK

I live across most of Australia, and have learned to thrive in cities. I like open areas of ground with trees or light posts that I can perch on and observe what's happening in my territory. I often croak to my fellow ravens about it.

Try looking for me in the city, local park, or out in the bush. Even if you don't see my species, you may see another species of crow or raven!

LISTEN

I make a rasping, croaky laugh, *waah-waah-waaaaaaaagh*.

youngster

adult

Spot the difference: Can you spot the differences between me and my close relative, the eastern rosella? How many different colours can you see in my feathers?

CRIMSON ROSELLA

Platycercus elegans

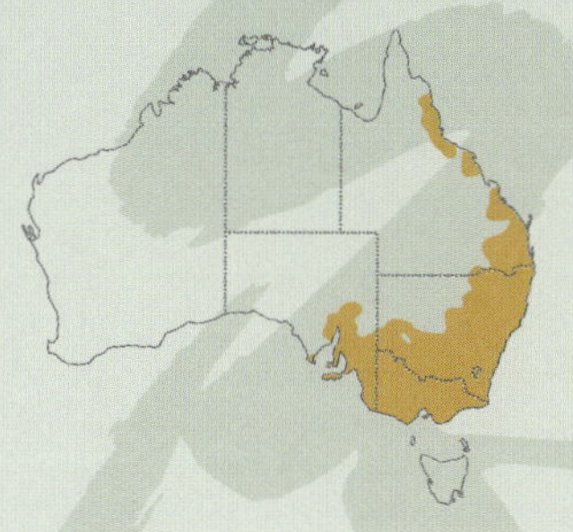

ABOUT ME

I'm a brightly coloured parrot who lives in lush gardens and bushland, especially in mountainous areas. I spend some of my time up in the tree canopy eating seeds, and I also like to waddle around on lawns where I can nibble on grass seeds and dandelions, which I find very delicious!

I spend my time with my life partner or in small groups. While my common name is crimson rosella, my colour is different in the drier, inland areas of Victoria and New South Wales, where I'm yellow instead of red. To make things even more confusing, when I'm a young bird, I'm mostly green (see opposite), then as I get older my feathers moult and I grow into my bright red and blue feathers.

When it comes time to breed I nest in tree hollows.

LOOK

I live in forests, lush gardens and parks across much of eastern Australia. I need big trees nearby to nest in.

LISTEN

I make a beautiful, bell-like call, *dwoop-dweeee*! I also chatter very sweetly when I'm munching seeds, or when I'm gossiping with my partner in the canopy.

DID YOU KNOW?

There are six different species of rosella in Australia! The crimson, eastern, northern, western, green, and pale-headed rosellas. All of them have beautiful colours, and live in different regions.

BIDJENAMBUL

[bi-djen-am-bul,
'dj' as in 'da**ng**er',
'u' as in 'p**u**t']
(Taungurung)

DID YOU KNOW?

The welcome swallow loves flying so much it doesn't even stop to drink – it just swoops down low and dips its beak into the water as it skims over it!

Spot the difference: Can you spot the differences between me and some of my relatives, the fairy martin and the white-throated needletail? We each have a different shape in the air.

fairy martin

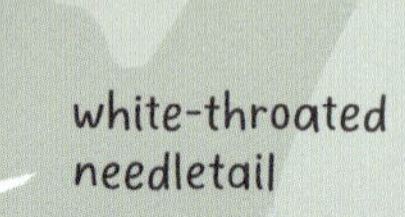

white-throated needletail

WELCOME SWALLOW

Hirundo neoxena

ABOUT ME

I'm a very fast bird who spends most of my life flying. Sometimes I zoom so fast, it's hard to keep your eyes on me! I often fly with a family group, usually over water or wet lawns where I can catch insects, even sometimes flying out to sea. I have whiskers around my beak that protect my eyes, and help direct insects into my mouth as I speed through the air.

My name comes from sailors, who knew that they were close to home when they started to see me visiting their ship. I have a rusty red patch above my beak and on my throat, but it's hard to see unless I pause to catch my breath on a powerline or fence. Mostly I'm silhouetted as I fly overhead, so I often look darker than I actually am.

I build my nests in sheltered places, often under people's roofs of houses, or among the struts under bridges, or on balconies in city apartment blocks. I build a cup-shaped nest using mud, straw and twigs.

LOOK

I live in lots of environments, including in the city, especially if there's a river or lake nearby. I often fly over or near water. Try heading to your local sports oval or park, especially after rain (or after the sprinklers have been on). This is when a lot of small insects will be active over the grass, so I often arrive in a small group to feed.

LISTEN

I make a high *seeep* as I fly, and a series of clicking calls.

male

female

Spot the difference: There are several black cockatoos who live in Australia. Can you spot the differences between me and the red-tailed black-cockatoo?

YELLOW-TAILED BLACK-COCKATOO

Zanda funerea

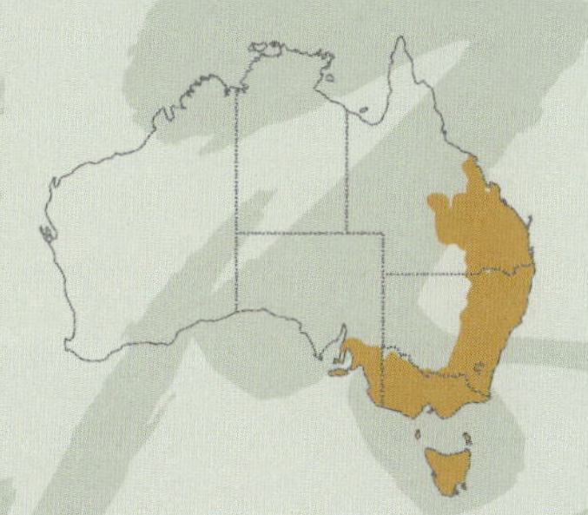

ABOUT ME

I'm a large black cockatoo, but despite my size you will usually hear my call before you see me! I fly with slow flaps of my wings, with my long tail straight out behind me, usually making a wailing call at the same time.

Like most parrots, I love to eat seeds, mostly from she-oaks, pine cones and gumnuts. I also eat some insects, tearing at wattles and other trees to dig out moth grubs that live in the wood. My beak is very strong, so I'm good at ripping open seeds and tree branches to get at the food inside.

I need old trees with big hollows to nest in. Only the females of my species incubate the eggs, while the males provide food to the females. Males have a pink ring around their eye and a dark beak, while females have a grey ring and a paler beak.

LOOK

I live in bushland, both in rainforest and drier woodland areas. I particularly love seeds from pine trees, so I often visit pine plantations with a big group to feed on pine cones. I also love sugar gums, which are my traditional nesting habitat. Try looking for me when you're near pine trees, or out in the bush.

LISTEN

I make a high-pitched, descending wail, *weee-wahh*, which is a bit screechy. I often repeat this as I fly.

NWERNINGK
[NOORN-ingk],
IYNEYNWENGK
[ee-NEEN-oongk]
(Alyawarr)

Spot the bird: Can you find me in the picture on the opposite page? See how well camouflaged I am?

TAWNY FROGMOUTH

Podargus strigoides

ABOUT ME

Many people think I'm an owl, but I'm actually in the group of night birds known as frogmouths. Like an owl, I like to sleep during the day and wake up at dusk, but I have a different body shape to owls, and I have a special wide bill. This is where I get the name frogmouth from.

At night-time I fly around hunting little critters like mice and frogs. I also catch moths, beetles and other insects. During the day my streaky brown feathers help me blend in with the tree trunks and leaves where I rest. I make myself even more invisible by staying as still as a statue when I sense a threat. I have striking yellow eyes, but often roost with my eyes closed.

When it comes time to nest, I build a loose platform of sticks in a tree, where I lay my eggs.

LOOK

I survive well in cities that have tall trees nearby, so try looking for me in green suburbs or parks. I also thrive in bushland areas.

Sometimes at night I fly around streetlamps because big moths are drawn to light, so they're easy for me to catch.

LISTEN

I often call at dusk, and occasionally around sunrise. I make a deep but soft *whoom* that I repeat over and over, like a slow drumbeat.

Spot the difference: Can you spot the differences between me and another member of my family, the malleefowl? We both like to build compost mounds to keep our eggs warm.

AUSTRALIAN BRUSHTURKEY

Alectura lathami

ABOUT ME

I love to dig through leaf litter in rainforests and backyards, finding insects to eat. I look a bit like a large chicken with a red head and a wattle at my throat (the yellow dangly bit). This wattle, and my red colouring, becomes much brighter in males during our breeding season.

I eat insects and grubs that live in leaf litter, but I will also eat fruit, food scraps and seeds. I can fly if I need to, but I'm pretty clumsy, so I only fly short distances.

LOOK

Sometimes I venture into suburban gardens, but only near wet bushland and rainforests, where there is plenty of leaf litter.

LISTEN

I make a deep, frog-like gulping noise, and a *whoooom* call that sounds a bit like an owl.

DID YOU KNOW?

When it's time to breed, male brushturkeys build a big mound of leaf litter. As the leaves break down, they release heat, so the mound becomes the perfect place to incubate eggs. The female then lays her eggs, and the male buries them to keep them safe and warm.

Male and female brushturkeys both have a heat-sensitive beak, kind of like a thermometer, so they can check the temperature of the mound by sticking their beak in it. When the eggs hatch, the chicks dig their way out of the mound and fend for themselves.

female

male

Spot the difference: Can you spot the differences between me and another Australian parrot, the gang-gang cockatoo?

GALAH

Eolophus roseicapilla

ABOUT ME

I'm a pink and grey cockatoo who lives all over the country. I usually sit in big gum trees, or graze on seeds on the ground. My back and wings are grey, but when I fly, you can see the flash of rosy pink on my belly.

I like to eat seeds from different plants and grasses, including from farmland, so farmers dislike me visiting because I eat their grain before they can harvest it! Other parrots also do this, including sulphur-crested cockatoos and corellas (*see* p. 19).

I'm a playful and social bird, feeding and roosting with my flock. When it comes time to breed, I use a tree hollow, so I need old-growth trees nearby to survive.

LOOK

I prefer to live in drier, open bushland, but I can also live in suburbs and towns that have big trees and water nearby. I often feed on the ground, but when it's hot I hang out in shady tree canopies to stay cool. Try looking for me in parklands, near sports ovals and golf courses, or in open bush.

LISTEN

I make a high-pitched, faintly screechy *chipp-chipp*!

DID YOU KNOW?

Male and female galahs look almost exactly the same, unless you can get a close look at their eyes. The females have red eyes, and the males have dark brown. When you next see a galah, try to spot which is which!

AREPEYLP

[u-REP-eelp,
'U' as in 'CL**U**MP'
or 'ER**U**PT']
(Alyawarr)

Spot the difference: Can you spot the differences between me and the masked plover? We both like to spend time on suburban lawns.

BUSH STONE-CURLEW

Burhinus grallarius

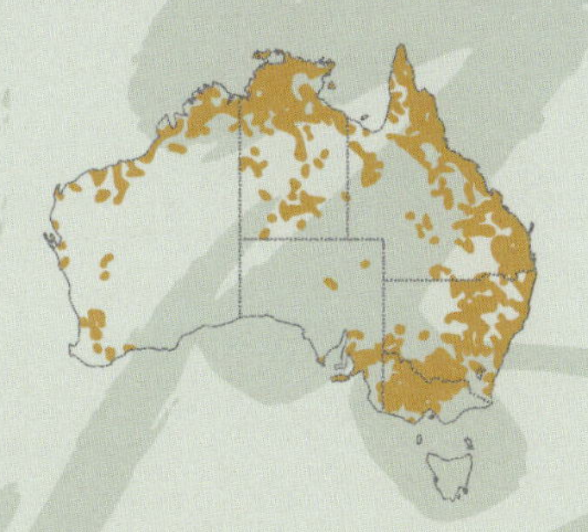

ABOUT ME

I'm a slow-moving, watchful bird who stalks around the suburbs on my long legs. I like to live in a small family group, usually roaming around the grass looking for insects and other small critters to eat, including skinks and frogs.

My colouring is quite plain, mostly brown and grey, so when I freeze (which I'm very good at doing) I blend in to my background. Although I move around and feed a bit during the day, I'm most active at night. My large eyes help me see in the dark.

When I find a mate, I choose a site on the ground where I lay my eggs, then guard them. I raise my newly hatched chicks by ushering them around the suburbs, teaching them to fend for themselves. If you approach my chicks, I'll puff myself up and spread my wings to try to scare you off.

LOOK

I live across much of Australia but am very common in suburbs in the warm tropics. I wander around lawns, golf courses and open bushland in a group, so keep an eye out where there's grass!

LISTEN

I make a very spooky-sounding whistle that rises then falls, *waaa-aaaargh*. Often I do this with my friends and family at night. I don't mean to be scary, but I might give you a fright!

Spot the difference: I'm one of several lorikeets who live in Australia. Can you spot the differences between me and the musk lorikeet?

RAINBOW LORIKEET

Trichoglossus moluccanus

ABOUT ME

I'm a brightly coloured, noisy and cheeky parrot. I love to drink nectar from flowering gum trees, grevilleas and banksias, where I gather with a family group. I have a special brush at the tip of my tongue that helps me lap up nectar from flowers.

Sometimes a tree I'm feeding in can be very noisy, because I'm fighting over flowers with other parrots and honeyeaters! Because I love sugar, if I get the chance I'll also eat fruit (things like apples, peaches and plums) and whole flowers.

I'm very acrobatic when feeding, so sometimes you'll see me swing upside down and clamber sideways through a tree to work my way from flower to flower. I'm a bit like a circus performer! When it comes time to nest, I lay my eggs in a tree hollow.

LOOK

I'm successful in many places in Australia, including suburbs and cities. Look out for me at your local park, or any place where there are lots of native flowers blooming.

If you have fruit trees growing in your garden, I might pay them a visit. Get in quick, or I might eat all the fruit before you do!

LISTEN

I'm almost always chattering or screeching to my fellow rainbow lorikeets. My most common call is a high-pitched, rising *qwiiiii*.

DID YOU KNOW?

Scientists recently discovered that there are actually multiple rainbow lorikeet species! One is called rainbow, and another red-collared. The map on this page shows the distribution of them both.

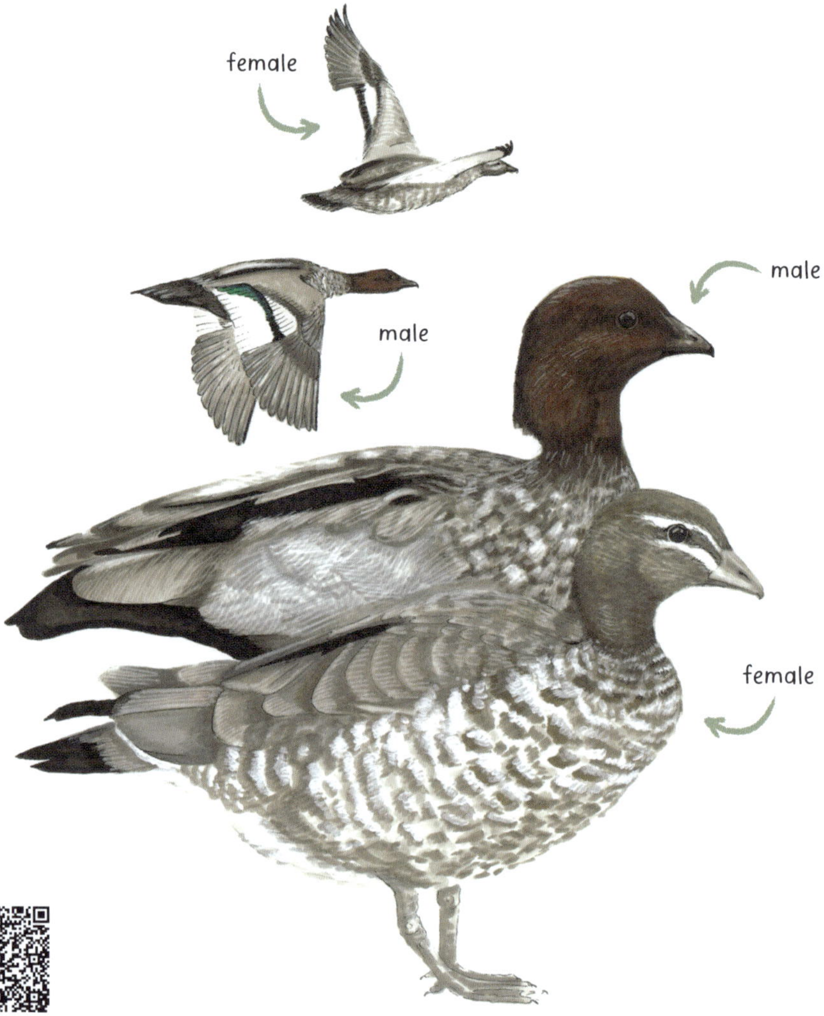

female

male

male

female

Spot the difference: I sometimes share habitat with another Australian duck, the Pacific black duck. Can you spot the differences between us?

AUSTRALIAN WOOD DUCK

Chenonetta jubata

ABOUT ME

I'm a beautifully patterned duck who hangs out in large groups. Males have a chestnut brown head, and females have a paler brown head with a white line above and below the eyes.

Occasionally I'll paddle on lakes and dams, but I mostly spend my time grazing on the ground. I feed on seeds and insects, though I also enjoy tender greens, like lettuce. Sometimes I sneak into a human's veggie patch and gobble it all up! I'm a generalist, which means I eat a lot of different things.

When it comes time to have chicks, I find a mate, and together we search for a tree hollow in which to nest. You might see me sitting on a tree branch chattering to myself, which I often do when I'm looking for a hollow. Once the eggs have hatched, my chicks need to jump out of the tree and drop several metres to the ground, where I'm waiting for them. How brave!

LOOK

I like to live in green suburbs, especially where there are plenty of lawns, ovals and parkland where I can feed. In early spring, try looking for me in bushland reserves or in large trees where I'll be searching for a nesting hollow.

LISTEN

I make a loud *heeeynk* noise, and sometimes I make a soft *enk-enk-enk-enk*. If you come too close to me or my mate – especially when we have chicks – I might hiss at you.

Spot the difference: Can you spot the differences between me and my cousin, the southern boobook?

POWERFUL OWL

Ninox strenua

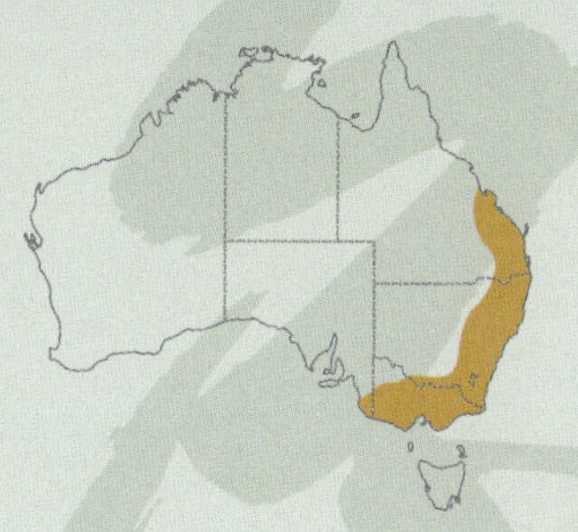

ABOUT ME

At around 60 centimetres – or two rulers – tall, I'm Australia's largest nocturnal bird. My wingspan can be nearly a metre and a half across! I'm patterned with brown and white chevrons (little arrows) across my belly. I have huge, round, yellow eyes which help me see in the dark.

By day, I roost in large trees with a thick canopy to keep me hidden. By night, I fly silently, hunting ringtail possums, rats, mice, gliders, other birds and the occasional brushtail possum. My enormous talons help me seize prey and carry it back to my perch, where I slowly devour it with relish.

I choose a partner for life, and when it comes time to nest I seek out a large tree hollow. Once my eggs hatch, I raise my chicks until they are strong enough to hunt and fly on their own.

LOOK

While I live in bushland and rainforest areas, I also venture into cities to visit botanic gardens and parks – anywhere that there are possums to eat!

Your best chance of seeing me is when I'm roosting in thick canopies during the day. Keep an eye out for me if you're visiting your local botanic gardens – I may be roosting in one of the trees!

LISTEN

I make a large, impressively deep 'hoot' call, *whoo-whoooot*. It is similar to the southern boobook, though my call is deeper.

NOW IT'S TIME TO VISIT SOME BIRDS THAT LOVE TO BE IN, ON OR NEAR THE WATER! YOU MIGHT SEE THESE BIRDS AT A BEACH, LAKE, OR CREEK NEAR YOU. WHICH ONES HAVE YOU SPOTTED?

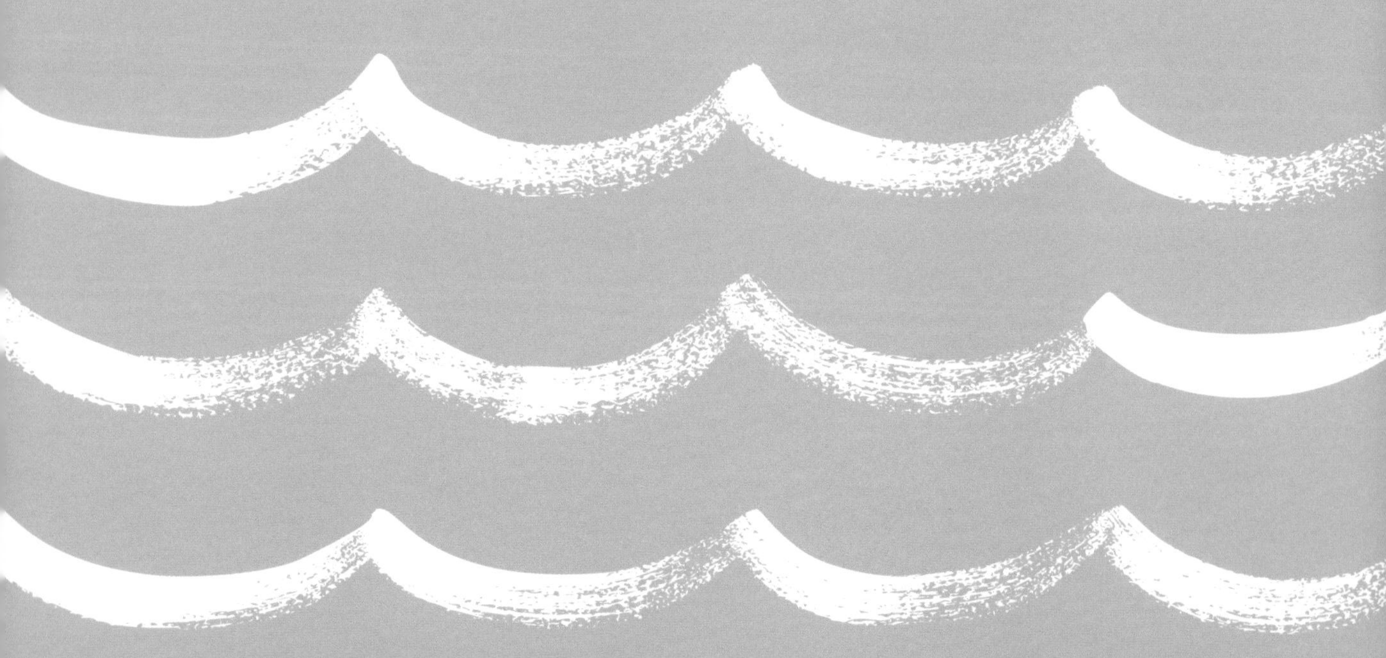

Water Birds

DID YOU KNOW?

The white ibis has learned how to eat poisonous cane toads without getting sick! These introduced toads have toxin-filled sacs that kill the creatures that eat them. The ibis has learned to shake these toads in its beak, forcing them to release their toxins. Then they wash the toad in water before eating them. What a clever bird!

Spot the difference: Can you spot the differences between me and the rare Far Eastern curlew?

AUSTRALIAN WHITE IBIS

Threskiornis molucca

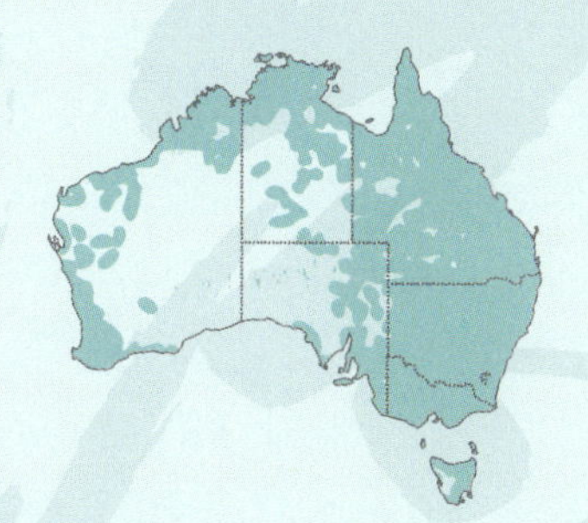

ABOUT ME

I'm a large wading bird with a long, curved beak that helps me look for food in shallow water and wetlands. My traditional habitat is in marshlands where there are lots of critters for me to eat, though I have adapted well to living in suburbs and cities. In these urban areas I wander on grass, feeding on food scraps and insects. When it comes time to nest, I build a platform of sticks in a large colony of nests shared with other ibises.

Sometimes people call me a bin chicken, but I think that's a bit rude! I prefer to be called a 'generalist' because I eat lots of different things. My main natural foods are insects and crustaceans, along with other small aquatic critters, such as fish and frogs.

LOOK

I prefer to live along the coastlines of Australia, but I can live anywhere with enough water and food. Try looking for me at local lakes and rivers, or even your local sports oval or parkland. Wetlands or farm dams are other good places to keep an eye out.

LISTEN

My most common call is a *honk*. At other times you may hear me making a clucking noise.

WALAYMPERR

[WAL-aim-per]
(Alyawarr)

JUNGGAARR

[joong-gar]
(Gumbaynggirr)

Spot the difference: Can you spot the differences between me and the yellow-billed spoonbill?

AUSTRALIAN PELICAN

Pelecanus conspicillatus

ABOUT ME

I'm a big waterbird who spends most of my time paddling in rivers or calm beaches. I have a huge, sensitive bill which I use to catch fish. The bottom half of my bill is fleshy and stretchy, so I can use it like a net to scoop up prey. You might spot a wriggling fish in my bill just before I tip my head back and swallow it! Although I mostly eat fish, I also eat yabbies, shrimp, crabs, skinks and sometimes I even eat other birds.

I'm a graceful flier, and will often soar up very high, sometimes with several pelicans in a V shape. I like areas where there is lots of food and water, so when inland lakes fill up I sometimes appear there in a large flock.

Before breeding, I make a nest either on the ground or in shrubs near water, layering sticks and debris to create a platform for my eggs.

LOOK

I'm always near water, so try looking for me at your local beach, lake or river. I often hang around areas where people go fishing, hoping they might throw me some of their catch! Sometimes I manage to snatch fish guts from the gutting bench – tasty!

LISTEN

I make a variety of grunting, croaking calls, *gakk-gak-gakk-gak*.

DID YOU KNOW?

Did you know that, like many other seabirds, the silver gull can drink seawater if it needs to? They have a special gland in their nostrils that removes extra salt from their bloodstream, making sure they have a healthy balance of water and salt in their body. It's like a built-in filtration system!

adult

youngster

Spot the difference: Can you spot the differences between me and another seabird, the Pacific gull?

SILVER GULL

Chroicocephalus novaehollandiae

ABOUT ME

You probably know me simply as a seagull, but if you look closely, you can see the silvery coloured wings that give me my name. Young gulls have a mottled brown pattern over their wings and back, which eventually turns into the silvery grey back of adults.

When it comes time to nest, I fly to offshore islands or rocky seaside outcrops where I build a shallow cup of sticks on the ground. Many other silver gulls will do the same close by, so we make a loud, busy area with lots of nests. In fact, my species tend to dominate these nesting areas, making it hard for other seabirds to raise their young there.

Traditionally, I eat animals found by or in the sea, including fish, insects and shrimp. However, I now eat a wide variety of human foods too, especially food that is littered or given freely in parks or on beaches. I'm very partial to chips, though they are not very good for me!

LOOK

Even though I traditionally live by the sea, as humans have changed the landscape I have spread far and wide, and learned to thrive in many inland areas and cities.

I spend a lot of my time on shores, in city parks where people feed me, and in the back alleys of markets or at landfill sites where I look for scraps among the rubbish.

LISTEN

I make a harsh, growling call, *trrowwwr*.

BIYAWIINY

[be-a-ween]
(Gumbaynggirr)

Spot the difference: Can you spot the differences between me and another member of the rail family, the dusky moorhen?

PURPLE SWAMPHEN

Porphyrio melanotus

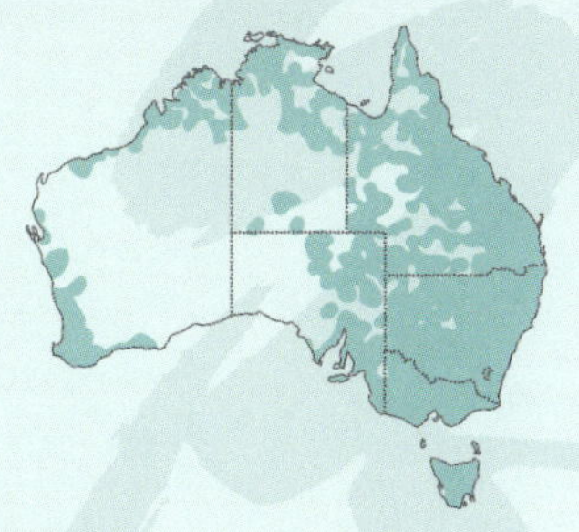

ABOUT ME

I'm a chicken-sized waterbird, and I spend most of my time stalking around lakes and ponds. As I move I flick my tail up and down, flashing a white patch on my bottom. (Humans still haven't worked out why I do this – they're not very bright!)

I'm a member of the rail family, a group of birds with long legs who often live in wetland habitats, looking for food in or near water. I particularly love hanging out in places with tall rushes and reeds, where I can stalk around unseen by predators.

I mostly feed on aquatic plant matter and little critters, such as grubs, lizards and frogs. Sometimes I eat other birds if I can catch them.

When it comes time to nest, I bend reeds and layer grasses and vegetation into a platform near or over shallow water. All of my family members contribute to raising the young, and defending the nesting site.

A tip for all you budding birdwatchers – in some books, you might see me named 'the Australasian swamphen'.

LOOK

I live across a lot of Australia, but I'm always close to water. Try looking for me at your local pond, lake or creek. You may see me walking along lake foreshores with other rails, like the dusky moorhen or the Eurasian coot.

LISTEN

I make a high-pitched *cluck*, and also a shrill screech, *neeerk*, that echoes over the water, letting you know that I'm somewhere close by.

Spot the difference: Can you see the differences between me and another large waterbird, the magpie goose?

BLACK SWAN

Cygnus atratus

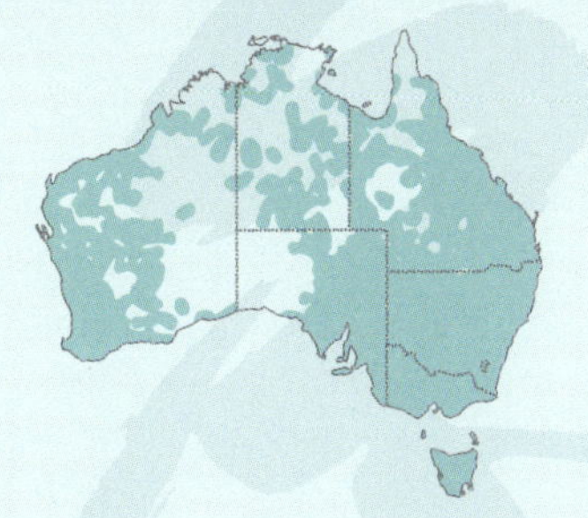

ABOUT ME

I'm a large, elegant waterbird who spends my time paddling on lagoons and beaches. Most of my body is black, with a white strip of feathers on each wing and a bright red beak. When I fly it is often in a group, with our long necks stretched out in front of us. When there is plenty of food and water in an area, we gather in large flocks, making for a spectacular sight.

I make a nest of folded reeds and grasses near or on shallow water, where I care for my eggs. Both the males and females of my species incubate the eggs and raise the chicks. I'm very protective of my cygnets (baby swans), so keep your distance, otherwise I might chase you off!

I eat algae and aquatic plants by dunking my head and chest underwater, and stretching my neck out to nibble them off the lake or river floor. You might see my backside poking out of the water while I feed!

LOOK

I live across a lot of Australia, but I'm always close to water. Try looking for me at your local pond, lake or creek. I sometimes even hang out in the shallows at sheltered beaches. Surf's up!

LISTEN

I make a varied *honk* call, sometimes shrill, sometimes soft.

DID YOU KNOW?

Each year after breeding, black swans moult and then spend around a month growing new feathers. They can't fly during this time, so they stay by a lake with plenty of food where they can wait for their new feathers to grow.

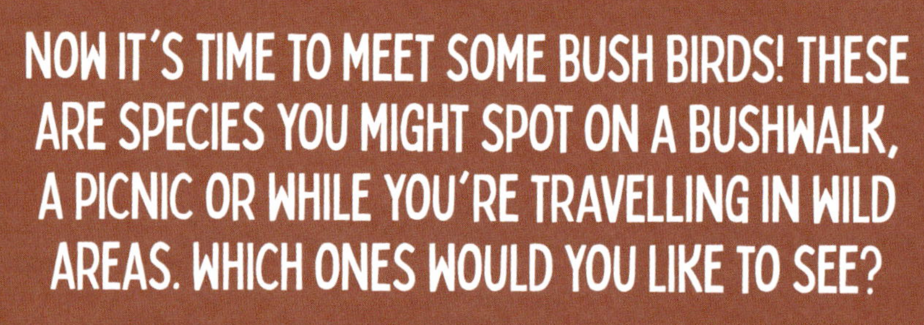

NOW IT'S TIME TO MEET SOME BUSH BIRDS! THESE ARE SPECIES YOU MIGHT SPOT ON A BUSHWALK, A PICNIC OR WHILE YOU'RE TRAVELLING IN WILD AREAS. WHICH ONES WOULD YOU LIKE TO SEE?

Bush Birds

DID YOU KNOW?

Cuckoos are very lazy and lay their eggs in other birds' nests so they don't have to look after their own chicks! To make sure that a cuckoo hasn't laid any eggs in its nest, fairy-wrens teach their unhatched chicks a 'code song' which they repeat back after hatching. By doing this, they make sure they are only feeding their own chicks. How smart!

Spot the difference: Can you spot the differences between me and the brown thornbill?

SUPERB FAIRY-WREN

Malurus cyaneus

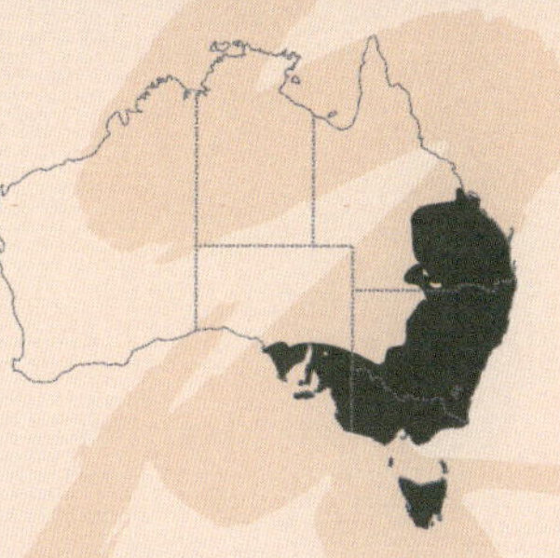

ABOUT ME

Most people remember me because of my spectacular blue feathers. Despite being very tiny and delicate-looking, I'm a bold, busy bird. I have a long, narrow tail which I keep upright as I hop around on grassy lawns or in shrubs, chasing insects to eat, like small beetles and flies.

I like to hang out in a big family group, where we all feed and spend time together. We look quite different from each other but we are all members of the same species. The young male birds are brown, the leader male birds are blue, and the female birds are brown with red feathers around their eyes. These different coloured feathers help us tell each other apart.

I like to have thick, dense grasses or shrubs nearby, so I have a safe spot to fly away to if I get scared.

When it comes time to nest, I build a cave-like dome of twigs and grasses for my eggs. I often build this in shrubs or tall reeds where I can nest safely away from predators.

LOOK

Even though I'm brave, I need lots of native vegetation to keep me safe and happy, so I mostly live in thick gardens and bushland. Try looking for me at your local park, or near a lake or creek.

LISTEN

I make a fussy *diwwii-diwwii-dirrrr* noise as I feed and gossip with my family.

Spot the difference: Can you notice the differences between me and another small forest bird, the silvereye?

WHITE-BROWED SCRUBWREN

Sericornis frontalis

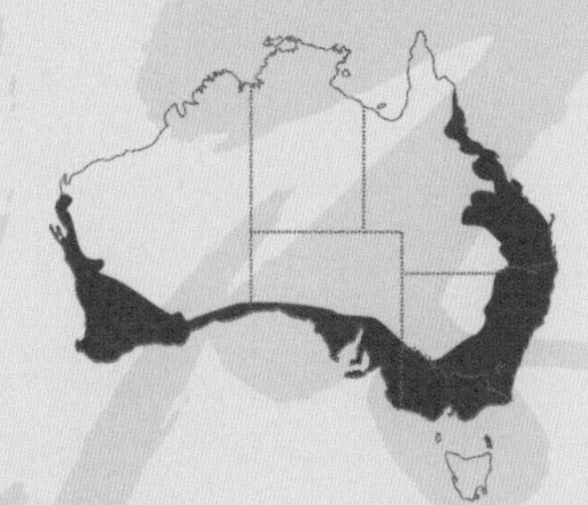

ABOUT ME

I'm a tiny brown bird who lives most of my life in shrubs and spiky bushes, where I can hop around chasing insects. My name comes from the bright white eyebrows I develop when I'm an adult.

I live in a small family group, gossiping and chatting to my fellow scrubwrens. I have lots of relatives in Australia who look similar to me, like the brown thornbill and brown gerygone (pronounced jeh-ree-go-nee). Sometimes all of us little brown birds hang out together in what is called a 'mixed feeding flock'.
We feel safest in a big group!

When it comes time to breed, I make a dome-shaped nest, which protects my eggs. My family members (including the teenagers) all help out with raising the new chicks, gathering and sharing food. This is called 'co-operative breeding' because
we all work together to look after the youngsters.

LOOK

I need dense shrubs to both nest and shelter in. Try looking for me where there are thickets. I'm usually close to bush reserves or in rainforests.

LISTEN

I make lots of different calls, but my most common and recognisable call is a 'scolding' sound, *pshh-pshh-pshh*. I also make a sweet, high-pitched whistle, *seeep-seeep-seeep*.

DID YOU KNOW?

Lyrebirds can mimic pretty much anything! They can pretend to be any other bird species – a cockatoo, magpie, kookaburra or whipbird – but they can also mimic humans talking, and even things like chainsaws!

BULN BULN

[buln-buln, 'u' as in 'put'] (Taungurung)

Listen to me: Using the QR code, listen carefully to my call. Can you hear me mimicking the yellow-tailed black-cockatoo? You'll have to be patient!

SUPERB LYREBIRD

Menura novaehollandiae

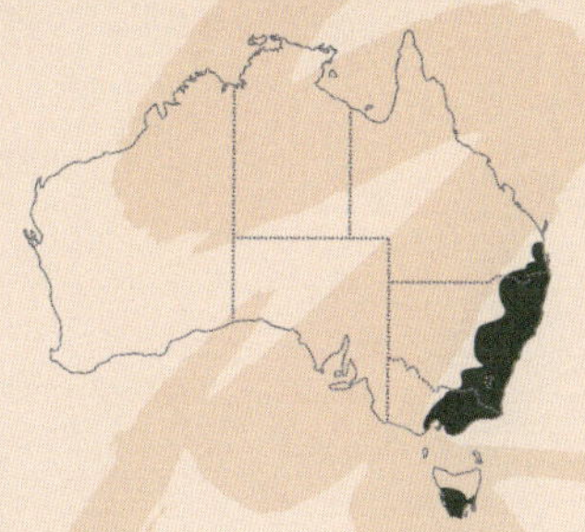

ABOUT ME

I'm a forest bird who is a big copycat! I'm an excellent singer and I'm very good at mimicking other sounds that I hear in the forest. I copy other birds as a way of showing off how clever I am to my fellow lyrebirds.

When I'm not practising my singing, I walk around the forest, digging through the soil, looking for insects and other critters to eat. Because I spend my time turning over the leaf litter and dirt, I mix all of the nutrients and microorganisms on the forest floor together, and this helps compost the soil. When the soil of the forest is healthy, that helps the plants and the animals that live in that forest to be healthy too. In this way, I'm important to many creatures in the forest. You're welcome!

I'm named for the shape of my tail when I lift it in the air, which looks a little bit like an instrument called a lyre, not because I 'lie', or pretend to be other things.

LOOK

I mostly live in rainforests and wet coastal bushland areas. I like to find open gullies above creeks where my calls echo loudly to everyone in the area. Try keeping an eye out for me when you visit the bush.

LISTEN

Because I'm so good at copying other sounds, it can sometimes be hard to tell if I'm a lyrebird, or if I'm the bird that I'm mimicking! If you listen carefully, between the different sounds I copy I also make a *bliikk-bliikk* call. If you hear this, then it's a pretty good bet that it's me who's singing!

DID YOU KNOW?

Did you know that wedge-tailed eagles will sometimes work in pairs to hunt kangaroos? That's double trouble!

IRRETY

[i-REACH]
(Alyawarr)

BUNDJIL

[bun-djil,
'dj' as in 'da**ng**er']
(Taungurung)

Spot the difference: There is another Australian eagle that is almost as big as me, known as the white-bellied sea-eagle. Can you spot the differences between us?

WEDGE-TAILED EAGLE

Aquila audax

ABOUT ME

I'm Australia's largest bird of prey with a wingspan of more than two metres – that's as long as a double bed! I'm named for my tail, which is wedge-shaped. This is easiest to see when I'm flying.

I spend a lot of my time soaring high up in the sky. As I fly, I save energy by finding air currents and warm thermals to float on, so I rarely have to flap my wings.

My eyesight is so accurate that I can spot prey from over a kilometre away! If I see an animal that I want to eat – like a rabbit, fox or wallaby – I will dive down to catch it using my huge talons. I also feed on carrion (dead animals), including roadkill.

When I nest, I build a platform of sticks high in a tree. I will sometimes build a nest in big powerline poles, where I can use cross-struts to support my nest.

LOOK

Because I'm an excellent hunter and can eat pest species that are widespread (like rabbits), I can live in lots of places. However, I do often fly over farmland and areas of dry, open bushland where prey is easy to spot. Keep an eye on the skies around these areas and you may get to spot me circling high overhead.

LISTEN

I very rarely call, but when I do, I make a sound a bit like a seabird: *ga-kaaah, ga-kaaah.*

DID YOU KNOW?

When it comes time to breed, male emus do all the child care. They incubate the eggs for nearly two months, often going without any food or water. After the chicks hatch, the dads teach them how to forage for food, and even how to find where it has rained and new food will be growing!

ANHELENGKW
[u-NEL-oongk],
ANKERR
[un-KER-a],
ARRANG
[u-RUNG,
'U' as in 'CL**U**MP' or
'ER**U**PT']
(Alyawarr)

BARRAMUL
[barr-a-mul,
'rr' is rolled]
(Taungurung)

Spot the difference: Can you spot the differences between me and another flightless Australian bird, the southern cassowary?

EMU

Dromaius novaehollandiae

ABOUT ME

I'm proud to tell you that I'm the biggest bird in Australia! You might see me from a distance when I'm walking through grasslands or open bushland.

Although I cannot fly, I do still have very small wings, which you can see at the sides of my body if you look carefully. Instead of flying, I use my long, strong legs to move around on foot, wandering far and wide in search of food. I particularly like seeds, fruits, plant shoots and insects.

My long shaggy coat looks more like fur than feathers. This is because my feathers are 'double plumed' – where most birds have one feather, I have two! (How awesome am I?) This helps my body trap air, allowing me to insulate myself (control the temperature of my body).

LOOK

I live in many areas across Australia, but I'm more easily seen in open grasslands and mallee (dry, open bushland). I can be hard to spot, so it's extra special if you spot me!

LISTEN

I rarely make a sound, but when I do, it's a drum-like *thump-thump-thump*.

DID YOU KNOW?

While the emu is the biggest bird in Australia, standing around 180 cm high, the smallest bird is the weebill, which is only 8 cm long and around 4 cm high!

CITY BIRDS BINGO

How many of these birds can you see in the city?

Australian white ibis

Raven

Noisy miner

Common myna

Common starling

Spotted dove

Rock dove (feral pigeon)

House sparrow

Silver gull

SPECIES CHECKLIST

BACKYARD BIRDS

- [ ] 1 Australian magpie
- [ ] 2 Pied currawong
- [ ] 3 Laughing kookaburra
- [ ] 4 Red wattlebird
- [ ] 5 Noisy miner
- [ ] 6 Eastern spinebill
- [ ] 7 Willie wagtail
- [ ] 8 Crested pigeon
- [ ] 9 Sulphur-crested cockatoo
- [ ] 10 Australian raven
- [ ] 11 Crimson rosella
- [ ] 12 Welcome swallow
- [ ] 13 Yellow-tailed black-cockatoo
- [ ] 14 Tawny frogmouth
- [ ] 15 Australian brushturkey
- [ ] 16 Galah
- [ ] 17 Bush stone-curlew
- [ ] 18 Rainbow lorikeet
- [ ] 19 Australian wood duck
- [ ] 20 Powerful owl

WATER BIRDS

- [ ] 21 Australian white ibis
- [ ] 22 Australian pelican
- [ ] 23 Silver gull
- [ ] 24 Purple swamphen
- [ ] 25 Black swan

BUSH BIRDS

- [ ] 26 Superb fairy-wren
- [ ] 27 White-browed scrubwren
- [ ] 28 Superb lyrebird
- [ ] 29 Wedge-tailed eagle
- [ ] 30 Emu

BUCKET-LIST BIRDS

- [ ] Little penguin
- [ ] Peregrine falcon
- [ ] Satin bowerbird
- [ ] Spotted pardalote
- [ ] Rainbow bee-eater
- [ ] Southern cassowary
- [ ] Eastern curlew

These are some other birds you might see if you're lucky!

GLOSSARY

Adapted: (see 'evolve')

Anther: The part of the flower that holds the pollen.

Bank: A slope of earth, such as a riverbank.

Burrow: A tunnel, sometimes with a wider 'cave' at the end, that is used by birds and some other animals (such as platypus) to nest in.

Canopy: The uppermost branches and leaves of trees.

Characteristics: A feature that is shared by the members of a species. For example, a long, curved beak, or a brush-tipped tongue.

Climate change: Unstable weather and temperature patterns across the planet, mostly caused by the increased levels of carbon pollution in the air from things like plane and car exhaust.

Colony: A group of the same animal living or nesting close together. Emperor penguins are a species who raise their chicks in colonies in Antarctica with thousands of other penguins. Safety in numbers!

Crest: Feathers on top of a bird's head.

Descendants: The children and children's children of an animal, including humans. You are the descendant of your family before you!

Ecosystem: A community of animals, plants, fungi, rocks and other elements of an area.

Embryo: An early stage of a lifeform. For example, an unhatched chick starts as an embryo. You started as an embryo too!

Environment: An area in which animals and plants live.

Evolve: The development of certain features over time that make it easier for a species to survive. For example, birds evolved feathered wings which allowed them to fly, helping them to find food and shelter more easily.

Germinate: The start of a new life form. For example, when a seed germinates, it starts to grow a shoot, which grows into a plant over time.

Habitat: The type of area where an animal lives. For example, a lyrebird may live in a rainforest habitat, which has lots of ferns and high rainfall.

Incubate: To keep eggs warm and protected so that the chicks can develop. Most birds do this by sitting on top of the eggs and covering them with their feathers.

Microorganisms: Small forms of life, including bacteria and fungi, that do important work in the environment. Microorganisms often break things down into smaller parts, making it easier for plants and animals to use. For example, some fungi break down wood into smaller parts, helping turn it into soil.

Moult: Losing feathers. Birds generally moult once a year, growing new feathers to replace the old ones.

Nocturnal: Active at night (unlike humans, who are usually active during the day, which is called 'diurnal').

Omnivorous: An animal that eats both meat and plants.

Oxygen: A molecule (small particle) that we and many other animals, including birds, need to breathe to survive.

Pollution: The build-up or dumping of waste materials that are harmful to the environment, for example, plastic pollution.

Porous: Like a sieve, a porous surface lets molecules of a certain size cross through the surface, while preventing others from crossing through.

Predator: An animal that catches and eats other animals for food.

Roosting: A term used for resting or sleeping. Lots of birds choose to sleep ('roost') on high branches in a tree canopy where they feel safe.

Species: A group of animals that are all very similar, sharing the same characteristics. For example, the rainbow lorikeet is a species. Its close relative, the musk lorikeet, is a different species with slightly different characteristics (smaller, with different colours, *see* p. 36).

Wetlands: An area where there is lots of water, either from a river system or from nearby ocean tides. Also known as a 'marshland'.

RESOURCES

Atlas of Living Australia: The Atlas of Living Australia is an app where you can record sightings of what you see in nature. You can mention any animal, plant or fungi.

ala.org.au

Aussie Bird Count: An event run every year in October where people from across the nation count as many birds in their backyard as they can.

aussiebirdcount.org.au

Birds in Backyards: Run by Birdlife, this website is filled with resources on birds that you can see in your backyard, including videos, identification guides and tips on creating habitat in your garden.

birdsinbackyards.net

eBird: An app to make bird lists that are shared worldwide. Look on eBird to find out which birds you might see in an area you're going to visit.

ebird.org/region/AU

RED WATTLEBIRD

BLACK SWAN

Field guides: If you've practised birdwatching and want to learn more, here are some info-packed field guides:

Field Guide to the Birds of Australia by Ken Simpson, Nicolas Day & Peter Trusler (Viking Press)

The Field Guide to the Birds of Australia by Graham Pizzey & Frank Knight (HarperCollins)

The Australian Bird Guide by Peter Menkhorst, et al (CSIRO Publishing)

Live stream of the Collins Street peregrine falcons: Around August each year, a live stream is available online showing the favourite nesting place of the peregrine falcons that live on 367 Collins Street in Melbourne, Victoria.

facebook.com/groups/peregrinesmelbourne

youtube.com/@367collinsfalcons4/streams

Protecting our night birds: Some rat poisons are dangerous to owls and other night birds if they eat a rat or mouse that has consumed that poison. This Birdlife Australia page tells you which rodent poisons are safe to use and which aren't.

actforbirds.org/what-to-buy-and-avoid

ABOUT THE AUTHOR

Hi there! My name's Georgia and I love to make art and to write about nature. I live in the Dandenong Ranges in Victoria, where I'm surrounded by trees and birds. I love birdwatching because of all the things birds can teach us about the world around us. I hope that by sharing these amazing animals, you will have learned to love birds too.

ACKNOWLEDGEMENTS

Many thanks to everyone who helped make this book, including Amanda Louey, Tahlia Anderson, Lauren Carta, Irma Gold, Hannah Janzen, Siena O'Kelly, Emily Maffei, David Blackman, Fred van Gessel, Alex Maisey, Olive, Noah, Brett, Viv and Orien.

Alyawarr names were provided with the help of David Blackman, Australian Society for Indigenous Languages (AuSIL), from his combined work with Dr David Moore, University of Western Australia, and Dr Jennifer Green, University of Melbourne. Alyawarr Country is in north-eastern central Australia, and includes an area crossed by the Sandover River, which extends towards the Plenty Highway in the south and the Barkly Highway in the north.

Gumbaynggirr names were provided by Muurrbay Aboriginal Language and Culture Co-operative in Nambucca Heads, New South Wales. The Gumbaynggirr Nation is located on the mid-north coast of New South Wales. Its southern edge is the Nambucca River, its western edge lies in the Great Dividing Range, and its northern edge is the Clarence River.

Taungurung names were provided by the Taungurung Land and Waters Council, in Broadford, Victoria. Taungurung Country is found in central Victoria. It includes the area between the upper reaches of the Goulburn River and its tributaries north of the Great Dividing Range. The western boundary extends from Kyneton, along the Campaspe River to Rochester in the north-west, eastward to Mt Buffalo and beyond Mt Buller, and from Benalla in the north down to the top of the Great Dividing Range.

eBird: Distribution maps were compiled using data from eBird (ebird.org), accessed in March 2020. Distribution patterns of species shift over time. Species names in this book were also taken from eBird.

Published in 2026 by Hardie Grant Explore,
an imprint of Hardie Grant Publishing

Hardie Grant Explore (Melbourne)
Wurundjeri Country
Level 11, 36 Wellington Street
Collingwood, Victoria 3066

hardiegrant.com/explore

A catalogue record for this book is available from the National Library of Australia

Hardie Grant acknowledges the Traditional Owners of the Country on which we work, the Wurundjeri People of the Kulin Nation and the Gadigal People of the Eora Nation, and recognises their continuing connection to the land, waters and culture. We pay our respects to their Elders past and present.

For all relevant publications, Hardie Grant Explore commissions a First Nations consultant to review relevant content and provide feedback to ensure suitable language and information is included in the final book. Hardie Grant Explore also includes traditional place names and acknowledges Traditional Owners, where possible, in both the text and mapping for their publications.

Hide and Beak
ISBN 9781741179378

10 9 8 7 6 5 4 3 2 1

Publisher
Amanda Louey
Project Editor
Lauren Carta
Editor
Irma Gold
Proofreader
Susan Keogh
Design and Typesetting
Hannah Janzen
Head of Production
Simone Wall

Colour reproduction by
Splitting Image Colour Studio

Printed in China by LEO Paper Products LTD.

The paper this book is printed on is from FSC®-certified forests and other controlled sources.

FSC® promotes environmentally responsible, socially beneficial and economically viable management of the world's forests.